FOCUSING ON
GOD

31 DAYS OF GOD'S GLORY AND GRACE

BY

FRANK HAMRICK

FOREWORD BY JASON EHMANN

D1508977

PositiveAction
BIBLE CURRICULUM

Focusing on God: 31 Days of God's Glory and Grace
by Frank Hamrick

Copyright © 2013 by Positive Action For Christ, Inc., P.O. Box 700, 502 West Pippen Street, Whitakers, NC 27891.

www.positiveaction.org

Printed in the United States of America

ISBN: 978-1-59557-163-2

Edited by C.J. Harris
Design by Shannon Brown

Published by

Contents

Focusing on God

First: A Vision   9

God's Blueprint for Your Life   10

Wrong Focuses—Part 1   11

Wrong Focuses—Part 2   13

The Right Focus—God   15

God the Father

God Is Omniscient   19

God Is Omnipresent   21

God Is Omnipotent   23

God Is Eternal   25

God Is Immutable   27

God Is Glorious in Holiness   29

God's Love   30

The Lord Jesus Christ

The Preciousness of Christ   33

Christ and the Tabernacle   35

The Purpose of the Incarnation   36

A Meeting of Two Kings   37

Mary Magdalene at the Tomb   38

The Ascension of Christ   39

The Holy Spirit

Who Is the Holy Spirit   43

The Ongoing Work of the Spirit   45

The Holy Spirit Teaches Believers   47

The Grace of God to the Believer

The Diversity and Unity of the Bible   51

Christ Is Our Righteousness   52

What Salvation Accomplishes   54

The Palace Beautiful   55

Trust Follows on the Heels of Knowledge   56

The Peace of God   57

Preparing to Bear Fruit   58

God's Glory—Our Treasure   59

The God of the Impossible   60

The First Claim Principle   61

Foreword

Reading the works of Frank Hamrick is much like reading the journal of an explorer whose mission is to uncover the world's greatest treasure. In his pursuit, Frank discovered the most awesome site he'd ever seen—a site not only worth the journey, but also worth revisiting again and again. What did he find? God Himself.

Just one glimpse of God's glory forever altered the course of Frank's life and teaching. Because of this, his writings reflect a singular focus—magnifying the majesty of God. "God has written His Book with a single overriding story," says Hamrick, "the Story of His Glory."

Like Frank, our highest ambition should be seeking God's glory and grace through all things—to see His light and run toward it. God's glory shines through the perfection of His Word, the majesty of His creation, and the radiance of Christ, who is the full expression of His glory. Without God's divine light, we grope blindly in the dark for meaning and value. But as we behold the glory and grace of God, the God-shaped void placed in our hearts at birth is filled to capacity.

Through the writings and ministry of Frank Hamrick, I've come to learn that this life isn't really about me—or anyone else—but about God. My prayer is that this 31-day devotional will be a tool that awakens your mind and heart to God's glory. May He cause His grace to overflow in your life, filling your heart and spilling over into the lives of others.

Jason Ehmann
President, Positive Action For Christ

FOCUSING ON
GOD

First: A Vision

(The Inner Man, Chapter 3)

When Moses saw God, he bowed his head and worshipped (Exo. 34:8). In spite of all of his learning and training in Egypt, he was struck by God's power and glory. He spoke boldly before Pharaohs in Egypt, but he trembled and bowed before a mighty God.

His countenance was also changed. Exodus 34:29–35 describes the shining face of Moses after forty days with the Lord. The very glory of God had left its impact on Moses' countenance! Godliness shows in one's face. Neither can godliness be hidden; it shows. You can't fake it, and you can't hide it. When you've been with God, your appearance will be changed.

When Isaiah saw God, he immediately cried, "Woe is me!" (Isa. 6:1–8). He saw his sin and utter unworthiness to face God. Then he became willing to serve. He surrendered his life in verse 8. He was so smitten by God that he would do anything God wanted.

Joshua's first reaction was to fall on his face and worship (Josh. 5:13–15). His second reaction, like Isaiah's, was a submissiveness to serve the Lord.

Thus, we see that in each episode in the Word the pattern is the same: first, the vision, then self-abhorrence followed by self-abasement, worship, surrender, service, and a changed life.

God's Blueprint for Your Life
(Behold Your God, Chapter 1)

God the Father has planned our holiness, and it is to this end that we are saved (Eph. 1:4). In fact, God planned our holiness before He created the world! Looking at the illustration, we see that God drew (diagrammed) the entire plan of our bringing glory to Him by *being holy* and *doing holiness*. Note the rest of God's plan in the following points.

Christ came to earth to provide the means for our holiness (Titus 2:14). Christ did not come to earth to save us from our sins! He came to make us holy! He died for our sins because that was necessary to accomplish His purpose. To say that Christ died only to save us from sin is to come short of God's real purpose of sending Christ. Therefore, man must be liberated from sin through the cross to be free for God to start him on the road to holiness.

Have you gone through the door of the cross? Have you been washed in the blood of Christ and redeemed (freed) from the curse of sin? If you haven't, trust Him now because God's plan requires everyone who brings Him glory to come by way of the cross.

The Holy Spirit performs, or perfects, our holiness. Ezekiel 36:26–27, though speaking of Israel, is an example of what happens to a Christian when he trusts Christ. The Spirit enters him to cause the believer to walk in God's statutes and to keep and do God's judgments. Thus, the Spirit comes into every believer and personally supplies him the power to be holy and to perform holiness. As we submit to Him, He does His work in us.

Wrong Focuses—Part 1

(*Behold Your God*, Chapter 2)

Second Corinthians 3:18 likens the Word of God to a glass or a mirror. What you see when you look in that glass is all-important. When men read the Word of God, they might see a number of different things. And what they see is perhaps the thing that they consider to be the most important thing in their life. It's critical that we focus on the right things when we read the Bible.

Focusing on Holiness

The 1800s witnessed a growing interest in personal holiness. Great holiness meetings and conventions sprang up all over England and America. A veritable "holiness" revival occurred. Men searched the Word to discover every possible truth on the subject. They preached and practiced the Word with fervency. This phenomenon continued well into the twentieth century. Then, around 1925 (shortly after World War I), some men began to attack the Bible. The rise of Higher Criticism and German Rationalism brought to everyone's attention the importance of the inspiration of the Word. As religious critics began to throw mud at the mirror of God's Word, Christians began to take a closer look at the mirror itself.

In the 1800s when men focused on holiness, several problems began to emerge. The holiness emphasis caused men gradually to become "feeling" or "experience" oriented. As more people were caught up with "being holy," they placed increasingly less emphasis on evangelism. As one lady of that period stated, "I've become so thrilled with this glorious holiness teaching that I seem quite beyond any interest in meetings just for the converting of sinners!"

J. Sidlow Baxter stated, "Beyond a doubt, the all-too-frequent diverting of the holiness movement from earnest evangelism became a definite factor in the ensuing deterioration." The problem was not in being holy; the problem was a wrong focus.

Focusing on the Word

But later Christians gained a new focus. Rather than focusing on holiness, their emphasis shifted to subjects concerning the Word itself. "Inspiration," "doctrine," and the "authority of the Word" became the watchwords of Christians. Men scrutinized the mirror. They analyzed it, dissected it, and defended it. For the next fifty years, the Bible itself became man's primary focus.

But again, the focus was on the wrong thing. Men were studying the Bible for merely the sake of study! This is what has no doubt led to the dead orthodoxy of our day. Many teenagers know all of the facts of the Bible, but they have little excitement about the Lord. Many of them can name all of the doctrines and use all of the right theological terminology. They might know the answers to all of the criticisms concerning the doctrine of inspiration. Yet, they have little joy and delight in the things of God. Their hearts seem cold. Our churches are not winning souls to Christ.

Wrong Focuses—Part 2

(Behold Your God, Chapter 2)

Continued from the previous devotion.

Focusing on Love

O ther people look into the Word and see only one word—love. Their thinking is completely colored by this word. Although Christians certainly are to love one another with the love that God has for us, there is a danger in focusing on love as the object and purpose of the Christian life. When love becomes our focus, we tend to develop a "hypocritical sentimentalism" that is sometimes expressed in oozing, syrupy-sweet, compromising practices. We tend to overlook sin because we don't want to appear to be "unloving." We let the message of God's hatred of and judgment against sin be drowned out by the message of His love.

Focusing on Rules and Laws

Some people seem to see the rules and regulations of God's Word above everything else. Their focus is on the "do's" and "don'ts" of God's Word. A segment of Jewish society in Jesus' day—the Pharisees—was guilty of this wrong emphasis. Although rules and regulations are certainly found in God's Word and should be known and obeyed, one becomes very pharisaical when he makes these the primary focus of his life.

Focusing on Doing

Still other people tend to focus on accomplishing great deeds. They emphasize the importance of witnessing, preaching, singing, tithing, faithfully attending church, etc. Christian duty is important, but it is not to be that on which a Christian is to focus. No one is to serve simply for the sake of duty or service. This wrong focus can lead to legalism, or the tendency to judge one's salvation by his or her performance of deeds.

Focusing on Being

Finally, some people are convinced that we are to focus our attention in God's Word on what we are to be. We have already pointed out that God is more interested in what we *are* than in what we *do*, but we are still mistaken if the only reason we study the Word is to *become*. A person may concentrate on being the right kind of person and still not be right with God. This focus can lead simply to self-improvement.

Summary

We have examined six things that of themselves are wonderful and desirable in a Christian's life: holiness, a right view of the Word, love, rules and laws, doing the right things, and being. Yet, a person can do all of them—seek to practice holiness and separation, know all the facts of the Word, manifest a spirit of love toward all men, know and follow all the rules and regulations, do all the right things, and develop wonderful character traits and inner qualities—and still not be right with God! Each of these areas can lead to a wrong conclusion if it becomes one's primary focus in life.

The Right Focus—God

(Behold Your God, Chapters 1–2, 4)

Note that God the Father planned our holiness (1 Pet. 1:15–16). Christ, the Son, provided the way for our holiness (Eph. 5:26–27). And the Holy Spirit performs that holiness in us (Eph. 3:16). As God looks down upon us, He sees that our primary goal is holiness. This is the goal He has set for us. This is the reason He created us. This is the target for which we are to be aiming, the goal we are to be striving to obtain. But although our goal is holiness in heart and action, our focus is to be upon knowing God, not upon holiness itself. Our focus is to be on a Person.

We have a right focus when we concentrate on a Person through the Word and Providence. The Pharisees studied the Word, but they failed to see the Lord in it! The Pharisees looked into the Word and saw only the rules and regulations, not the glorious Person of the Word. But we are to read and study God's Word that we might discover the Lord. We also come to know the Lord through the instrument of Providence. Providence is every event and circumstance that occurs in our life from birth to death. God intends to use all these events to glorify Himself and manifest His goodness towards us.

Remember these three important points.

- Our goal is holiness.
- The means to holiness is love.
- The focus is on knowing God.

All three of these points are important, but knowing God is the initial step. As we focus on knowing God, we develop a deeper love for Him, which then makes us holy.

Jeremiah 9:23–24 says, "Thus saith the Lord, Let not the wise man glory in his wisdom…"

Don't glory in the fact that you might be smarter than other people, that you can memorize Scripture faster than other people, or that you can read faster or score higher on the quiz without much effort. Don't glory in those things.

"…neither let the mighty man glory in his might…"

Don't glory in the fact that you might be bigger or stronger or prettier than other people or that you are a good athlete or maybe even a sports hero.

"…let not the rich man glory in his riches."

Don't glory in your fine clothes, your flashy new car, or your big, well-furnished home.

Don't glory in any of these things. "But let him that glorieth glory in this, that he understandeth and knoweth Me, that I am the Lord which exercise lovingkindness, judgment, and righteousness, in the earth: for in these things I delight, saith the Lord."

GOD THE
FATHER

God Is Omniscient

(Behold Your God, Chapter 11)

The word *omniscience* comes from two Latin words meaning "all" and "knowledge." Therefore, the omniscience of God simply means that God knows everything. God has never learned and cannot learn, for He already knows—and has always known—everything.

God knows everything—everything possible, everything actual; all events; all creatures of the past, present, and future. He is perfectly acquainted with every detail in the life of every being in heaven, earth, and hell.

God knows the number of hairs on our head (Luke 12:7). He even calls the stars by name (Ps. 147:4). He never discovers anything; He is never surprised, never amazed. He never wonders about anything. There never has been a time when there was anything that God did not know, nor will there ever be such a time. What a wondrous Being is the God of Scripture! As we learn of His omniscience, we ought to bow in adoration before Him. Yet, how little we do meditate upon this divine perfection.

Because God knows everything, He knows what is best for us, and we can trust Him to provide it. What a great blessing, comfort, and cause for joy this truth is for Christians!

Each person is a diamond in the rough. We have an inner beauty, inner qualities that God is seeking to bring out of us. But these qualities are hidden; we have rough edges. God must bring the chisel of people, circumstances, and things into our lives to knock off those rough edges and conform us to the image of Christ.

Let God do His work in your life. Don't resist the chisel. If you do, God will just get a bigger and sharper chisel! Don't question God's dealings with you. Rather, thank Him for dealing in your life. If God isn't working in your life, it is evidence that you are not saved. He knows what is best, and you can trust Him to provide it. You can rejoice, for you know that He is working in your life to make you like Christ.

This truth is often easy to put into our heads, but it is very difficult to put into our hearts. Yet, once it sinks into our hearts, it will greatly change our attitudes and actions. There are few truths that will affect our conduct as much as this one. When we are in the midst of a "bad" situation, our tendency is to complain and gripe. Never do that!

We can trust God! Someone once remarked that he wanted to know what God had in store for him, what was at the end of the road for him, what he would be doing in five or ten years. But that's not God's way.

We don't need to know the future. We need to know only Him who knows and plans the future and to trust Him to give us His best. Let this truth sink into your heart. Live upon this knowledge of God. God knows what is best for us, and we can trust Him to provide it.

God Is Omnipresent

(Behold Your God, Chapter 12)

The word *omnipresent* means "all present." God is present everywhere. The story is told of a missionary to India who found Hindu worshippers tapping on various trees and stones and asking, "Are you there?" They were looking for the presence of their god. The omnipresence of God means that He is everywhere at one and the same time. He is in Mexico at the same time He is in Australia. He is on board every ship on the high seas, in every airplane in the skies, and in every spaceship in outer space—all at the same time.

The Bible makes it clear that no one can escape God. Jonah is one of the best illustrations of this truth. Jonah, God's own prophet, should have known better than to try to run from God. Surely he knew that it is impossible to escape the Lord. God is the Lord of the sea and could deal with Jonah just as easily on the water (or in Tarshish) as on dry land (or in Nineveh). This shows how we often try to run from God.

From the examples of Jonah and Adam and Eve, we see the sheer folly of running or hiding from God. Yet, do we not find ourselves trying to do the same thing every day? We run from surrendering to Him and from being separated unto Him. We also try to hide our sins from Him.

God is everywhere, sees everything, and controls everything. God knows what is said at every terrorist cell meeting, as well as what is said inside of your church. He is present in every strategy meeting behind all the closed doors of the White House Oval Office. He can turn the heart of any king or ruler as simply as the waters are turned by the channel of a river (Prov. 21:1). Although God allows man to sin and make many foolish decisions, He is ultimately in control and works all things according to His master plan.

This same verse (Prov. 21:1) also indicates that God can do as He pleases in the hearts of all who are in authority any time He desires. Whenever our righteous intentions are thwarted by a person in authority, our first recourse should be to appeal to God in prayer to turn the superior's heart so that he will not block our righteous desires.

God is present in every believer. First Corinthians 6:19 and Colossians 1:27 express the fact that both Christ and the Holy Spirit indwell our bodies. Therefore, everywhere we go we take Him with us. You are chaperoned everywhere you go! He is with you in private, on a date, at every amusement, etc. Be careful where you take the Holy Spirit!

Finally, learn to practice the presence of God. Talk to Him everywhere you go. The heart of meditation is conversation with the Lord. There is no better way to be conscious of His presence than by talking to Him. First Thessalonians 5:17 admonishes, "Pray without ceasing."

The early Puritans had a way of seeing God in everything and practicing His presence. Every time they saw a flower, they said something like, "My, what a beautiful work of creation, God." "Lord, thank You for giving such a perfume to that flower for me to enjoy." They lived literally as though He were standing beside them in the flesh. And isn't He, really?

God Is Omnipotent

(Behold Your God, Chapter 13)

By the omnipotence of God we mean that He is able to do whatever He wills. God can do anything that is in harmony with His perfections. He cannot lie because He is truth. He cannot behold evil for He is pure and holy. God can do whatever He wills, but nothing that violates His nature. The word *omnipotence* appears once in the Bible and is used only of God (Rev. 19:6).

God's power was openly displayed when He became incarnate and tabernacled among men. To the leper He said, "I will; be thou clean. And immediately his leprosy was cleansed" (Matt. 8:3). To one who had lain in the grave four days He cried, "Lazarus, come forth," and the dead came forth (John 11:43). The stormy wind and the angry waves hushed at a single word from Him (Luke 8:24). A legion of demons could not resist His authoritative command (Luke 8:27–33).

All events that have ever transpired upon this earth have been in the control of God. Every earthquake, every flood, every hurricane, every tornado, every thunderstorm, every volcanic eruption, every rockslide, every fire, and every other event of nature is in the control of God. All human actions—whether past, present, or future—are dependent upon the power of God. Mark this fact: not a creature in the entire universe has an ounce of power except what God gives it (Rom. 13:1 and John 19:11). So we must never fret over the world situation.

God also has control over our personal problems. He is not merely sitting back in heaven as an idle and unconcerned spectator of the events in our lives.

Every one of us has some annoyance. It might be someone at school or on the job with whom we just can't seem to get along, or someone who just irks us. It might be someone who tries to get the best of us, who is a thorn in our side. It could be an enemy. Or it might be a circumstance—no car, hand-me-down clothes, a rundown house and neighborhood, or unsaved or divorced parents. It could be a problem involving personal appearance—too tall, too short, straight hair, curly hair, blonde hair, black hair, a big nose, a hooked nose, crooked teeth, or poor eyesight. Whatever it is, rest in this fact: God is in control. God has the power to change the situation—or to give you the ability to bear up under it.

The next time you are tempted to complain about a problem, ask yourself, "Is God omnipotent? Is God in control?" The inevitable answers to those questions will stop your complaining about people, circumstances, and things.

We have no power except that which God gives us. And yet, because He indwells us, we have all power and "can do all things through Christ which strengtheneth me" (Phil. 4:13). When God calls us to do something for Him, He will enable us to do it. You can do anything that is in the will of God for you.

God Is Eternal

(*Behold Your God,* Chapter 14)

To say that God is eternal is to say that He is infinite (without limitation) in existence. God is from everlasting to everlasting. He is the King eternal. Time has a past, a present, and a future, but eternity does not. God is a timeless Being. So when we think of God as being eternal, we think of Him as existing in an eternal present without past or future, an eternal today without a yesterday or a tomorrow. Although God is the author of time, He is in no way bound by it.

Because God is eternal, we know that the blessings He promises to His children are eternal as well. Our troubles and sufferings are short, but our reward is eternal. First Thessalonians 4:17 says that we shall "ever be with the Lord." The sunlight of glory shall rise upon the soul and never set. God Eternal shall eternally reward the saints.

We are now traveling the road of eternity. Whether we are awake or asleep, we are traveling the road. Some of us may be near the end of the road—on the border of eternity.

Think of your soul's eternity. You had a beginning, but you shall have no end. God has set eternity in our hearts. God has set a hunger in our hearts that the temporal cannot satisfy. Although the heart of the unbeliever was created with a hunger for God, he tries to satisfy himself with other things. He tries to satisfy himself with everything but God.

Jeremiah 2:13 describes the unregenerate heart: "they have forsaken Me the fountain of living waters, and hewed them out cisterns, broken cisterns, that can hold no water."

This man has an inner emptiness that creates a gnawing restlessness. He seeks to fill the emptiness with sports. He hungers and thirsts to be a great athlete. All of his time and energy are spent to this end. Some people seek after riches, and riches satisfy for a time. But they are like snow castles lying under the torrid beams of the sun. They are quickly gone. Other people seek to fill their emptiness with drugs, sex, and achievement—anything but God. Unsaved man will do anything to fill the emptiness. Never does a hungry man come with more eagerness to his food than a wicked man does to his sin. And when Satan sees men with such an appetite, he will provide a dish they love. He will set the forbidden fruit before them.

The unsaved can fill up the cistern and be satisfied temporarily, but the water quickly seeps out, and the thirst returns. It leaves behind the dregs of guilt, frustration, dissatisfaction, and lack of fulfillment. The real problem is not with what we put into the cistern; the problem is with the cistern itself. It is a faulty inner condition. We need a new cistern, a new self, a new nature. And that comes only by trusting Christ as Lord and Savior.

Christ said, "He that cometh to Me shall never hunger; and he that believeth on Me shall never thirst" (John 6:35).

Never thirst! Christ satisfies. Notice that in John 2, at the marriage feast in Cana, Christ performed His first miracle. When He ordered the servants to fill the empty water pots, they were filled to the brim. They lacked nothing. The emptiness was completely filled.

God Is Immutable

(Behold Your God, Chapter 15)

To say that God is immutable is to say that He is unchanging and unchangeable. He is perpetually the same. Deuteronomy 32:4 compares God with a rock, which remains immovable although the entire ocean surrounding it is continually fluctuating. Although all creatures are subject to change, God is immutable.

First, God is immutable and unchanging in His character. God's character has never grown or improved. His character cannot change for the better, for He is already perfect. Being perfect, He cannot change for the worse. Improvement or deterioration is impossible for Him. He is perpetually the same.

Because God is unchanging in His character, I can trust His person. This fact offers solid comfort. We cannot always rely upon our human nature, but we can always rely on God. However unstable or unsure I might be, however fickle and changing my friends might prove to be, God does not change. If He varied as we do, if He willed one thing today and another thing tomorrow, who could trust Him?

God is unchanging in His truth. How unreliable are the words of men. How often we have heard two sports opponents claim superiority, knowing that one of them must suffer defeat. How often political candidates have assured themselves and their followers of victory only to go down in defeat. How often candidates have made promises that they never fulfill. Even in business, men's words often are not to be trusted. We have created an entire network of contracts and legal systems to force men to be true to their word, yet men still lie and deceive one another. Truth seems to mean nothing to them, even in court under oath. How frequently nations fail to live up to their word in treaties. Examples abound throughout history.

God is unchanging in His ways. He always acts in accordance with unchanging principles. This consistency makes God predictable. We can predict what God will do because He is unchanging in His principles, and I can trust His principles. God is concerned not only with what we do but also how we do it. God is unchanging in His ways and principles. He will always honor those who do the right things the right way.

God is unchanging in His purposes; therefore, I can trust His plan. God is both omniscient (has perfect foresight of all things) and omnipotent (has all power), so He never needs to change His mind or reverse His plans on anything! God has planned to supply all of our needs. God plans to come one day for His saints. God's purposes have not changed and will not change, so we can trust His plans.

God's Son is unchanging. God the Father planned our holiness, God the Son provided the way to our holiness, and God the Holy Spirit performs the holiness in us. And because God the Son is unchanging, His provision for our salvation is unchanging; thus, we are eternally secure. Our provision for heaven is sure.

God Is Glorious in Holiness

(Behold Your God, Chapter 16)

We are living in a country today that has become profane. We have rebelled against God. We have become an ungodly nation. Although this country was founded on undeniably Christian principles, we gradually deteriorated until we became a nation that was Christian in name only. Today, many scholars refer to our times as the "post-Christian era"; we are no longer Christian even in name.

Why has this sad circumstance developed? We have forgotten the awfulness of God. God is awful. He is awesome. He is majestic. He is august. He is holy. But we have lost sight of this fact.

Exodus 15:11 tells us that God is glorious in holiness. Someone has said that "power is God's hand or arm, omniscience His eye, mercy His bowels, eternity His duration, but holiness is His beauty." God's holiness is the glory of all His attributes.

- His justice is a holy justice.
- His wisdom is a holy wisdom.
- His power is a holy power.
- His truth is a holy truth.
- His goodness is a holy goodness.
- God is glorious in His holiness.

When we take a photograph of someone, we don't want to see their hands or feet; we want to see their face. So it is with our vision of God. He desires us to see not His hand or finger, which denote His power and skill, nor even His throne as indicating His majesty. The way by which He wants to be remembered is by His holiness, which is the attribute that most glorifies Him.

Holiness is His name. (Read Psalm 111:9.) We don't find phrases such as "His mighty name," "His wise name," or "His loving name" in Scripture. But Scripture quite often reminds us of "His holy name." God is absolute purity. He is unsullied by even the shadow of sin. First John 1:5 says, "God is light and in Him is no darkness at all." God is glorious in holiness.

How casual and cavalier we are about this holy God. Our casualness demonstrates how little we know of what—and who—He really is.

God's Love

(Behold Your God, Chapter 19)

Definitions of the love of God are so many and varied that we almost hesitate to offer another. Yet, we must try to communicate an idea of what God's love is all about. Before we define God's love, however, we should perhaps define love itself. Love is simply that which seeks good for the object loved.

"But," some people might ask, "what is good?" Romans 12:2 provides our definition. Good is "the will of God." Knowing this allows us to complete our definition: Love is that which seeks the will of God for the object loved.

Dr. Rolland D. McCune defined God's love thus in his book *Basic Bible Doctrine* (Minneapolis, Minnesota): "God's love is that in God which moves Him to give Himself and His gifts spontaneously, voluntarily and righteously for the good of personal beings regardless of their merit or response."

The phrase "God is love" has been grossly misunderstood and misapplied by some theologians. To say that God is love is not the same as saying that love is God.

To equate love with God is a major mistake. Had the apostle declared that love is what God is, we would be forced to worship love itself as the only God. The phrase "God is love" means that love is an essential attribute of God, that God is the very epitome or embodiment of what love is. Love is something true of God, but love is not God.

J. I. Packer points out that "God is love" is not the complete truth about God so far as the Bible is concerned. We may never divorce any one of His attributes from His other attributes. To say that a God of love cannot also be a God of wrath and severity is to pervert the Bible and to make God a monster. A God who cannot hate or move in wrath is just as much a monster as a God who is all hate.

For example, suppose that a mother finds a poisonous snake lying in the crib beside the dead body of her baby. Would she be normal if she picked up the snake that had just taken her child's life and stroked it lovingly and wished it no harm? A being that loves must hate anything that would harm what He loves. Therefore, God must be a God not only of love but also of truth, justice, wrath, and severity.

The fact that God is love means that His love is expressed in everything He says and does. Therefore, we can apply Romans 8:28 to every circumstance. All things—not just some things—work together for our good. Everything that happens to a child of God is an expression of God's love to him or her and comes for the furthering of God's purpose.

THE LORD JESUS CHRIST

The Preciousness of Christ

(Behold Your God, Chapter 21)*

John Fawcett, a famous English Baptist preacher who was saved under the ministry of George Whitefield in the eighteenth century, wrote a book titled *Christ Precious.* In the opening pages, he stated, "Without a sincere attachment to the Author of eternal salvation, whatever works of morality we may perform, our obedience will be materially and essentially defective, as not flowing from a proper principle." In twenty–first century terminology, he is saying, "If one does not have a sincere love of Christ, all the service he or she performs for God is worthless."

God's greatest interest is not in what you do or what you know. His interest is in what you are. Christ's greatest question for His disciples was "Lovest thou Me more than these?" (John 21:15). He doesn't value our service unless our hearts are in it. He knows what is in man. He sees and judges the heart and regards no outward acts of obedience if devout affection does not motivate the acts.

It is not enough for our eyes to be lifted up to Him or for our knees to bow before Him. It is insufficient for us to use our tongues to speak of Him or for our hands to act in His service. The Pharisees did all of those things. We must first give Him our hearts. Paul wrote in Ephesians 6:24, "Grace be with all them that love our Lord Jesus Christ in sincerity."

First Peter 2:7 summarizes the true Christian's response to this expectation: "Unto you therefore which believe He is precious." The word *precious* signifies "honor, infinite value, great expense." Thus, we find Peter saying, "Unto you therefore which believe He is of infinite value, He is costly, He is like a precious ruby, He is honored as pure gold.

The sacred writers considered Christ as the all-in-all of their religion, and as such they loved Him with their whole hearts. If they wrote of the first tabernacle, they called it a "figure" of Christ. If they spoke of prophecy, they called Christ the very Spirit of it. If they spoke of the gospel, they talked only of Christ crucified.

All of the great doctrines of the Word center in Christ. Jesus said, "I am the way, the truth, and the life" (John 14:6). All truth finds its center and ground in Christ. Every writer in the New Testament emphasized this truth, as is evident when one reads the exhortations that they wrote on the various doctrines. The passages that are doctrinal in nature are filled with the words

Christ and Jesus Christ our Lord. Remove Christ from the center of these doctrines, and they fall apart.

All of the graces and comforts of a Christian reside in Christ. Philippians 1:11 and 2:1 emphasize the fact that the life of all the graces and comforts of a Christian in this world is found in Christ. For example, faith finds its resting place in Christ. (In nothing else will true faith lodge.) Repentance is produced by contemplating a dying Savior. Love is kindled by meditation on Him. Peace is grounded in knowing Him. Fellowship finds its basis in what He has done for us. And mercy does not exist apart from Him.

Truly, all of the fruits of righteousness find their very sap of life in the person of Christ. At the same time, sin loses its taste as one keeps his eyes on Christ, and the world loses its attraction when we love Him.

Without Him, all of these graces would wither and die because He is the ground, the sunshine, and the dew of their existence. The same sun that produces the fruit of righteousness will wither and burn the fruit of sin and worldliness. As the hymn by Helen Lemmel (1864–1961) says,

Turn your eyes upon Jesus,
Look full in His wonderful face,
And the things of earth will grow strangely dim
In the light of His glory and grace.

Christ and the Tabernacle

(The Life of Christ: From the Gospel of John, Chapter 5)

The Greek word for *dwelt* means "as in a tent," "tabernacled," or "pitched his tent." This translation involves the idea of temporary living quarters. For at least thirty-three years, Christ "pitched His tent" on earth as a man.

This translation reminds us of the ancient tabernacle of Israel in the wilderness. That tabernacle foreshadowed God the Son, incarnate on earth. Let's consider a few comparisons between the Old Testament tabernacle and Christ's incarnation.

1. The tabernacle was temporary.

So was Christ. He was with us for about thirty-three years and was constantly on the move. Similarly, studies of the Word show that Israel used the Old Testament tabernacle in the wilderness for less than thirty-five years.

2. The tabernacle was outwardly unattractive.

So was Christ. Read Isaiah 53:2: "He hath no form nor comeliness; and when we shall see Him, there is no beauty that we should desire Him."

3. The tabernacle was God's dwelling place.

God lived between the cherubim above the mercy seat. There, in the Holy of Holies, He manifested His presence by the shekinah glory. And during the years that the Word tabernacled among men, God dwelled in Palestine. On the Mount of Transfiguration (Luke 9:28–36), He flashed some of His glory. (Remember, God is light!) John was there and saw Him "glistening." He reminds us in verse 14 that "we beheld His glory, the glory as of the only begotten of the Father."

4. The tabernacle was where God met man.

God told Moses how to build the tabernacle and then stated, "And there I will meet with thee, and I will communicate with thee" (Exo. 25:21–22). Today, Christ is the meeting place between God and men. "No man cometh unto the Father but by Me" (John 14:6). (See also 1 Tim. 2:5.)

5. The tabernacle was the center of Israel's camp (Num. 2:17).

Even so should Christ be the center of our lives too. We should relate everything to Him.

The Purpose of the Incarnation

(The Life of Christ: From the Gospel of John, Chapter 5)

God has a purpose in everything He does.

To reveal the nature of God (John 1:18)

Until the birth of Christ, men had never seen God. They had seen theophanies, but they had never actually seen God. They had seen only God's handiwork in nature (Rom. 1:20) and read about Him in the Old Testament Scriptures. Now, however, God wants us to know Him intimately. (Note Heb. 1:1–3.)

The verb *declared* means "revealed," "interpreted," or "made known." This meaning gives us a clue as to why Christ was called "the Word." Through words we make our feelings known. Similarly, God made His feelings known to us through His Word. (See Heb. 1:1–2.)

Therefore, God is called the *logos,* or the expression of God.

To reveal the grace of God (John 1:14–17)

In the Old Testament, man saw God's law (given by God through Moses) and justice. God was gracious, however, even in the Old Testament; His grace just went unnoticed. Now God wants us to experience His grace fully.

He did not *have* to send Christ! We had deliberately transgressed; we were guilty and justly condemned. We deserved hell. Furthermore, man did not even *want* God's love and grace! Yet, God still sent Him to die for us. *That's* how the Incarnation reveals God's grace!

By way of illustration, suppose that someone stole from you and was caught. You forgive him and offer mercy, but he slaps you, curses you, and says that he doesn't want your mercy. That's exactly what man did to God, yet He *still* sent His Son!

To reveal the truth of God (John 1:14)

God loved us, but His truthfulness could not let Him overlook our sin. Sin had to be punished. So Christ came to bear the punishment for our sin. His agony on the cross reveals not only the grace and the truth of God but also the following three other truths:

- The awful consequences of sin
- God's hatred of sin
- The consequences that we must pay if we refuse the substitute

A Meeting of Two Kings

(The Life of Christ: From the Gospel of John, Chapter 27)

Pilate demanded to know the accusation against Jesus (John 18:29). The Jews offered none except to say that Jesus deserved to die (18:30–32). Pilate then took Jesus inside for a private conference (18:33–38).

At this private conference, two kings met: one was an earthly king and the other was a heavenly king. The ensuing conversation showed why Jesus is called the King of kings (refer to 1 Tim. 6:13–16). Pilate was no match for our Savior, and in a moment of awe and wonder he exclaimed, "Thou art a king, then" (18:37), to which Christ responded, "Thou sayest that I am a king."

Jesus made the "thou" in His statement emphatic to emphasize the point that Pilate had admitted that He was, indeed, a king. Jesus then stated that He had come into the world to "bear witness of the truth" and then added, "Every one that is of the truth heareth My voice."

Pilate responded, "What is truth?"

His question is interesting in light of what Jesus had just said. His question proved beyond a doubt that Pilate certainly was *not* of the truth because he did not understand what Christ had said. He had no idea what Christ meant by "the truth."

Mary Magdalene at the Tomb

(The Life of Christ: From the Gospel of John, Chapter 34)

One of the most touching scenes in the New Testament takes place in John 20:11–18. Mary Magdalene had come back to the tomb after telling the disciples that it was empty. It was still very early, and she stood beside the tomb weeping, not only because her Lord is dead but also His body has been stolen. What a moment she experienced when, as she turned from looking into the tomb, she saw a man standing nearby. He asked her why she was crying. Mary could not see well through her tear-filled eyes, and she assumed that the man was the gardener. She blurted out an anxious request for the "gardener" to tell her where the body had been taken.

We must remember that this was the same Mary who, as a demon-possessed woman, had been marched through the streets by men who bound her and made money off her. A few years before, her mind had been warped and twisted until she had met the Savior, who had simply spoken her name—as only He could speak it. She had never forgotten that day when her mind was made whole and the demons fled. From that day on, she worshipped the Lord, but now she would never hear that voice again—or so she thought!

Then suddenly she heard the "gardener" speak again. But this time He spoke her name, and He spoke it as only one person could speak it: "Mary" (20:16). And that one word was enough. What a moment it was as the sunlight of glorious realization burst upon Mary's soul. *He is alive! He lives forevermore!*

Our Lord is a living, risen Savior. Hallelujah!

The Ascension of Christ

(*Behold Your God,* Chapter 26)

There has probably never been a more spectacular event in all of history than the ascension of Jesus Christ into heaven. As dramatic as the resurrection was, it was witnessed by only a few guards, who fled in fear even before the actual appearing of Christ from the tomb. The ascension, by contrast, was accomplished in broad daylight with His disciples looking on. With no visible power or apparent effort, Jesus suddenly began to rise from the ground and ascended higher and higher until He disappeared into the clouds.

Imagine yourself a disciple at that moment! It has been forty days since the miraculous resurrection of Christ, and you have followed Him in awe, listening and learning everything He has said during that time. You and the other ten disciples are now gathered with Him near Bethany and the crest of the Mount of Olives. Suddenly, Jesus raises His arms to bless you. You have noticed that His words have sounded like a parting address. He has sounded as though He was getting ready to leave—but where would He go? You would follow Him to the ends of the earth. Now He begins to bless the small band of disciples.

Then, you notice something strange. In the midst of His heavenly benediction, He seems to be rising. Slowly, His feet lift off the ground. Your eyes dart up and down. You see no strings, no force lifting Him. You start to reach for Him, but something tells you not to interfere. As He rises higher, your natural instinct causes you to step back in awe. Your mind begins to whirl. What is happening? Where is He going? As He rises above your head, His eyes are at first still looking down, and His hands are outstretched as though He were giving you His final blessing. You fall to your knees in weakness and bewilderment. But then, He slowly lifts His head and raises His hands upward, and the clouds begin to envelop His body.

Now it begins to dawn on you: He is leaving earth for heaven. His earthly work is finished. His heavenly work now begins. By now, you are unable to see Him, and then, as though all of the others present were sharing the same emotions, the other ten disciples look at you and at each other. For one short moment, understanding passes between their gaze, and with one accord they face the ground and begin praising and worshiping the Lord. Oh, what prayers are uttered! The truth has dawned. His earthly ministry is now in your hands!

Moments pass. Joy fills your hearts. You have a great work to do. You must hurry to Jerusalem to proclaim what you have just seen. A world awaits the news, and you must tell them even though they will not believe. Some people will mock, others will hate, and still others will kill some of you. But still you must tell this news. The ascension is complete.

THE HOLY
SPIRIT

Who Is the Holy Spirit

(Behold Your God, Chapter 31)

The Holy Spirit is the Third Person of the Godhead and is equal with the Father and the Son in essence though distinct as a person. John 14:16 and John 16:7 refer to Christ's sending "another comforter." Two Greek words exist for the word *another*. One word means "another of a different sort," and the other word means "another of the same kind." We often use *another* in the same ways. For example, we might purchase a shirt and either dislike the color and say, "I want another shirt," meaning that we want another of a different color, or discover that the shirt has a hole in it and so say, "I want another shirt," meaning one of the same kind but without the hole.

The important thing to note in these verses is that the Greek word used here means "another of the same kind." Therefore, the Holy Spirit is the same kind as Christ. Because Christ is very much a person, so is the Holy Spirit.

The word *comforter* is the Greek word paraclete, meaning "called beside." It refers to someone who is called to stand beside another person to give him aid, to defend him, or to serve him as a lawyer. The same word is used of Christ in 1 John 2:1 when it is translated "advocate." Thus, we again see that the Holy Spirit and Christ are alike. Both are "paracletes." Now, who would want a paraclete (lawyer) who was not a real person? Therefore, as Christ is a personal Paraclete, so is the Holy Spirit.

Because the Holy Spirit is a person, He has emotions and can be mistreated. Ephesians 4:30 tells us that the Holy Spirit can be grieved. This means that the He mourns and cries. He can be hurt. A careful analysis of Ephesians 4:25–32 catalogs activities that grieve His holy soul. Most of these activities are connected with the use of our tongues and our inner attitudes. We must realize that the Holy Spirit is a person who has feelings and can be grieved and saddened by our speech and our attitudes.

Hebrews 10:29 tells us that the Holy Spirit can be insulted. When one rejects the Lord, it is a personal affront to the Holy Spirit.

Suppose that our government decided to rescue someone who had been taken hostage by a foreign terrorist group. After spending hours, weeks, and months planning the rescue operation, and after several of our soldiers had been killed and wounded in the rescue effort, the team finally reached the hostages.

"We're here to rescue you," the team leader declared to the hostages. "Let's get out of here!"

But suppose that the hostages then said to him, "We want to think about it first. Some of us really aren't interested in leaving."

What an insult that would be to the risks and dangers our soldiers took to free the hostages! Yet, that is exactly what we do to God's Spirit when He comes to rescue us from the condemnation of hell and we reject Him. Jesus Christ went to the cross, shed His precious blood, and endured untold agony of both soul and body for guilty, undeserving sinners. Then, the Holy Spirit comes to our hearts with news of our release, and we say, "Well, let me think about it!" or "I'm not quite ready yet!"

The Ongoing Work of the Spirit

(Behold Your God, Chapter 32)

The basic work of the Spirit in creation is to give life to the creation. Job 33:4 clearly indicates this fact. Obviously, what would creation be without life?

Imagine the Holy Spirit going forth to create and then returning to report to the Godhead that His work was completed. God peers out and sees the stars, the planets, and the earth—but no life anywhere! The earth is just that—earth. No grass, no trees, no food, no crops, no man. Imagine God saying, "Well, that's not exactly what I had in mind!" But because He is God, the Holy Spirit knew the thought of God the Father and gave life to creation.

In discussing the significance of the work of the Holy Spirit in creation to our lives, we must remember one overriding principle: The Holy Spirit's work in creation involves His activity in four areas—life, order, adornment, and renewal.

We must realize throughout that the Holy Spirit makes the difference in creation. He made the difference in the creation of the universe. He makes the difference in our lives. When we accept Christ as our Lord and Savior, we become the creation of the Holy Spirit. (See 2 Corinthians 5:17.) This universe is His creation, and He is thus active in all four areas of His creation. Even so, when we are saved, we become His creation and, thus, He is active in these same four areas in our lives. This is what is meant by our overriding principle.

He gives spiritual life to us. (See John 3:5, John 6:63, and 2 Cor. 3:6.) When we are born again, it is by the agency of the Holy Spirit. He becomes in a sense our "spiritual mother." Apart from the working of the Holy Spirit, it is impossible to be born again. The Father planned our salvation and the Son provided for it, but the Holy Spirit performs it. It is the Spirit that gives us spiritual life.

Isaiah 40:12 informs us of this work. When the Holy Spirit created this earth, He made everything in perfect proportion. He made an ecologically perfect environment: just the right amount of water, just the right amount of land, and just the right atmosphere. His work in creating this universe was so orderly that it is perfectly predictable. Astronomers can tell us where each heavenly body appeared in the sky four thousand years ago and where it will appear four thousand years from now. The Holy Spirit put such order into His universe that we can set our watches by its motions!

Job 26:13 says, "By His spirit He hath garnished the heavens." The word garnish means "to beautify or to glisten." The Holy Spirit was the one who adorned creation. All of the beauty and the glory of this earth was the work of the Holy Spirit. We see this beauty when we view the glory of the heavens; cascading waterfalls; rolling, green fields; snow-capped mountains; lush, green valleys; invigorating beaches; the multitude of natural wonders such as the Grand Canyon, the Redwood National Forest, and Luray Caverns; the beauty of the animal kingdom, the birds, the butterflies; and the beauty of man. All of this adornment and beauty was the work of the Holy Spirit. Remember the next time you are struck by the beauty of nature that beauty was put there by the Holy Spirit.

The Holy Spirit Teaches Believers

(The Christian Adventure, Chapter 7)

The natural man cannot understand the Bible. First Peter 1:10–13 tells us that even the prophets who recorded God's Word could not understand it, for it was not for them, and 1 Corinthians 2:14 states that the natural man cannot understand the Word. That is, man, in his natural state and without God, cannot understand the Bible.

For example, a dog or a cat cannot understand a ballgame on television (or anywhere else, for that matter). Why not? Because they are of a different nature than man. The Bible is a supernatural book, and only those who have a supernatural spirit can understand it.

Only by the Spirit can one understand the Word. First Corinthians 2:9–13 reveals that what the prophets did not understand and what the unsaved cannot understand, the saved man can understand—but only as the Holy Spirit teaches him.

1. He Teaches Us All Things (John 14:26)
We need the Holy Spirit to guide us as we read the Bible because it must be spiritually understood or discerned (1 Cor. 2:14). The Holy Spirit is specially equipped to teach us because He is the Author of the Scriptures (2 Pet. 1:21).

2. He Reminds Us of Forgotten Things (John 14:26)
The disciples who were to record Christ's life from memory several years later especially needed this reminder. How could they remember verbatim every conversation of Christ and the words of every sermon He preached? Only by the Holy Spirit. This point also shows the importance of Scripture memorization. If His Word is not in us, we can never recall it. But once we memorize it—even if we forget it—the Holy Spirit can bring it back to our memories when we most need it.

3. He Reveals the Future (John 16:13)
This fact was especially true for John, who would write Revelation at the age of 90! And it is true in us as God's Spirit enlightens our eyes to understand prophecy and to see it unfolding in daily events around the world.

4. He Teaches Us Especially of Christ (John 16:13, 14)

Some people who claim to have had a special charismatic experience say that they seek to glorify the Spirit. But God's Word teaches that when we are truly filled with the Spirit, we will glorify Christ, and our knowledge of Him will increase.

THE GRACE OF GOD TO THE
BELIEVER

The Diversity and Unity of the Bible

(Dynamic Christian Living, Chapter 7)

We must understand that what we know as the Bible is actually one book. We call this book the Bible because the English word Bible is based on the Greek word *biblia* (singular—*biblion*; plural—*biblia*). Although what we call "the Bible" is a collection of many books amid much diversity, it is also important for us to recognize that there is a sense in which it is nothing more than one book with one Author.

According to Hebrews 1:1–2, God has spoken to the world in various times. That means that God spoke to man through many different time periods (more specifically, over a period of more than 1,500 years—from about 1450 B.C. to about A.D. 100). God also spoke to man in different ways. Thus, God spoke to man through various media. For example, He spoke through visions and dreams, through angels, by direct oral communication, and in Moses' case, "face to face" (Exo. 33:11).

The Bible's diversity also extends to the number of human authors cited (around 40), the number of languages employed (three—Hebrew, Aramaic [very similar to Hebrew], and Greek), the types of literature featured (e.g., stories, poetry, legal code, prophecy, drama, satire, letters, visionary writings, proverbial sayings), and the variety of places and cultures where books were authored or sent (from Babylonian culture in modern-day Iraq to Roman culture in modern-day Italy). The Bible is made up of a very diverse collection of writings.

Yet through all the various ways in which God spoke to the Old Testament writers, there was really only one Author—the Lord. In Hebrews 1:2 God speaks of the New Testament as coming through His Son, Jesus Christ. Thus, all of our Bible is really one book written by one Author, and this accounts for its amazing unity.

The Bible is not a collection of stories that teach good moral truth. Rather, it is one story with one ultimate goal. Simply put, the Bible is the story of God's glory! The Bible begins with "God" (Gen. 1:1) and concludes with mention of God's grace (Rev. 22:21). The Bible is God's self-revelation. It is His autobiography! As such, we should read it to learn His story and His glory.

Christ Is Our Righteousness

(The Christian Adventure, Chapter 30)

When the sinner is convicted, he will try to escape the conviction. However, the poor sinner doesn't realize that he can't run. Once the gospel has been presented to him and conviction sets in, the Holy Spirit follows him wherever he goes.

A sinner can run from the preacher, he can stay away from church, he can avoid the soul-winner, and he can turn his television or radio from the preaching of the Word to something worldly. But he can't erase the Word of the gospel from his memory; he will take it with him wherever he goes.

In the book *Pilgrim's Progress,* the character Hopeful mentioned eight things that kept reminding him of the Word that Faithful, another character, had spoken to him.

- Every time he met a good man on the street, he remembered his own sinfulness.
- Every time he heard the Word, even in a conversation, the old conviction arose.
- Every time he got sick, he remembered that he was a sinner and would be judged.
- Every time a neighbor got sick, he remembered his sin.
- Every time he heard the funeral bells ring, every time he passed a cemetery, conviction rose in his soul.
- Every time he thought of dying, he naturally remembered his lost condition.
- Every time he heard of accidents or tragedies in other families, he remembered his own soul's tragic condition.
- Every time a thought of judgment entered his mind, the old conviction was rekindled.

From this we see the continuing power of the Word of God when a witness is given. A sinner can try to run all he wants, but God pursues him through his memory.

To escape conviction, a sinner might try to reform himself. He might join a church, give to charities (some of the largest charitable donations come from notorious sinners under conviction), or become active in humanitarian and philanthropic activities. These works seem to soothe his conscience for a while, thus giving him a false sense of hope.

In the story, Hopeful wondered, "How, then, can I be righteous?" His religious service didn't earn righteousness. Baptism wasn't the answer. How can a person be righteous enough to satisfy a holy God?

Faithful's answer was simple: Christ is our righteousness (Matt. 5:20; 1 Cor. 1:30). We do not get to heaven because of our deeds but because we have accepted Christ and His deed! It's as if we tell the gatekeeper at the Celestial City that we want to be admitted based on the righteousness of Christ. He lets us in, not because we are righteous but because Christ, in whose name we come, is righteous.

What Salvation Accomplishes

(The Christian Adventure, Chapter 8)

Regeneration

The first thing that salvation accomplishes is called regeneration, which means the same as "born again" and refers to the fact that the person whom God has saved is literally a new person inside; he has a new nature.

Redemption

Salvation also accomplishes redemption. This word means "to purchase," or "to buy back," and indicates that Christ has purchased the newborn person and now owns him. First Corinthians 6:19–20 shows the practical result of redemption. Because He owns us, we must live for Him rather than for ourselves. We become His possession and now exist for His glory alone.

Remission

The word *remission* means "to do away with" and indicates that our sins have been removed forever. The exciting thing about remission is that it covers all of our sins—past, present, and future. That is, when Christ died for our sins, He died for all of them, and when we accept His death as payment for our sin penalty, we accept payment for all of our sins. Thus, no sin that I can commit in the future can cause me to lose my salvation because those sins were totally removed by the Cross.

Justification

Justification means "declared innocent of sin and righteous before God." As a result of the remission of our sins, God sees us as completely innocent. Therefore, He declares us as righteous as Christ. We are now fit for heaven and God's holiness, which demands perfection, is satisfied and lets us freely enter heaven.

Glorification

Romans 8:30 tells us that the Christian is also glorified, that is, he has a new body waiting for him in heaven. In fact, in the mind of God, the Christian is already in heaven with the glorified body, for the word *glorified* in Romans 8 is in the past tense. Thus, God says that we are saved, justified, and—in His mind—already in our new, glorified bodies, worshipping Him around the throne!

The pilgrim is now sure of heaven. The only matters that remain in doubt are when he will get there and whether he will be a victorious or a defeated Christian when he arrives. All of the rest was settled at the cross.

The Palace Beautiful

(*The Christian Adventure,* Chapter 9)

*[The following passage describes Bunyan's allegory of struggles
faced by new believers seeking true Christian fellowship.]*

Leaving the Cross, Christian followed the narrow road and soon came upon three men sleeping. He tried to wake them, but soon he learned his first lesson after becoming a Christian—that not all men will be as zealous or as enthusiastic about their salvation as he was. This fact is generally a rude awakening for young Christians. The freshness of their newfound life is so exciting to them that they cannot imagine anyone who is truly born again being so lethargic.

Leaving these men to their slumber, he spied two pretenders to the faith (Formalist and Hypocrisy) trying to climb over the Wall of Salvation. He warned them that they must come in by the gate, but they were not interested in such talk and used tradition and ease as their reasons for climbing over some other way. Soon, however, they came to their end when they sought another shortcut around the hill Difficulty. So it often is with pretenders. They'd don't have what it takes when the way gets rough. That's why Jesus said, "If ye continue in my word, then are ye my disciples indeed" (John 8:31). These two men did not continue in the way and so proved that they were not of the way.

Christian headed up the hill Difficulty and after several problems (such as falling asleep and losing his roll), he finally arrived at the top of the hill and, shortly thereafter, at the Palace Beautiful.

Historically, this palace had its origins in a large house on top of Ampthill, near Bedford, England. Bunyan often went by this beautiful home and once stayed in it overnight. From the upstairs bedroom windows, one could look out and see in the distance the Chiltern Hills, which became the Delectable Mountains of *The Pilgrim's Progress*.

Allegorically, however, this palace becomes a symbol of the local church. Now that the pilgrim is a Christian, he needs the fellowship and teaching that the local assembly can provide. The fellowship he failed to find with the sleepers and with Formalist and Hypocrisy, he now finds in the local church body.

Trust Follows on the Heels of Knowledge

(Proverbs: The Fountain of Life, Chapter 34)

In Proverbs 3:6, we are called upon to acknowledge God in all our ways. The term acknowledge literally means "know Him." Here we are once more faced with meditation. Only by meditating on Him, on His character, on His providences, and on His glorious Person and work can we come to know Him, then live and trust Him, and finally submit totally to His will in our lives. Perhaps you are having trouble allowing God to have His way in your life because you don't really know God.

Trust must follow on the heels of knowledge. Trust takes the teeth out of Satan's lies. At the very heart of Satan's three lies is distrust of God. Satan tells us, "God wants to make you miserable, so be careful, don't let Him trap you! God's will is alright, but your own ideas are so much better!"

However, when we come to know and believe with all our heart that God does know what will make us the happiest, the most fulfilled, and the most successful and that He will see to it that this happens in our life, then all of Satan's lies are clearly foolishness to us.

When we trust God explicitly, when we know Him and commune with Him every day, He will direct our every step in the right path. That is, we won't even have to find God's will—it *will find us!*

Some sincere believers miss God's will because they are trying *to find God's will* rather than trying to *know God.* We must seek *God,* not His will. Finding God's will is a byproduct or result of walking with our mind and heart on only Him and serving Him. Every step we thus take is by faith and trust in God. And what does God do? He just keeps spreading His will in our path, so that no matter which way the believer turns, God's will is right in front of him. Thus, he can't miss being in God's will.

The Peace of God

(Proverbs: The Fountain of Life, Chapter 23)

Peace is realizing that God has provided all I need. We could probably shorten this definition further if we could grasp its full meaning: *Peace is realizing God! Thus, p*eace is nothing more than realizing that God is in charge of your life, that He is all-powerful, that He ever watches over you, that He never slumbers or sleeps, and that He will never allow you to suffer above what He wants and what He knows you are able to bear. All that happens to us is working together for our good (Rom. 8:28). Recognizing and living in light of this fact is the very essence of peace.

The first type of peace is peace *with* God. This upward-looking peace is necessary because of man's sin. Sin has placed man at enmity with God. Although God loves man, sin separates man from a holy God. God's wrath, stirred by man's sin and ordered to operate by God's justice, will not allow man to go unpunished. Therefore, unless man's sin can be dealt with, God's wrath and justice will condemn all men to hell. Thus, all men need to make peace with God.

This is where the cross comes in. Colossians 1:20 tells us that Christ made peace through His blood. That is, through His death on the cross, Christ paid for our sins and satisfied the demands of God's justice. Now that the price has been paid for peace, only one thing remains—faith in Christ.

God, the Holy Spirit, desires to produce in you the spiritual fruit of peace. This fruit grows best in the sunlight of meditation on God's character. As we came to God in faith at salvation and found peace *with* Him, so we must come to Him daily in faith to enjoy the peace that we have *in* Him.

We must also yield to God if we are to have peace with all men (Eph. 4:2-3). Sometimes that means biting our tongue. It may mean going to someone who has wronged us, and, rather than accusing them, apologizing to them for having wrong attitudes toward them. But, if we are to have peace, we must let God work in our hearts.

Preparing to Bear Fruit
(Proverbs: The Fountain of Life, Chapter 21)

When preparing to bear spiritual fruit, we must consider the law of adding and subtracting, or the principle of replacement, which is found in Colossians 3:8-10.

This passage calls on believers to put to death the thoughts and actions of the old man. This old man was governed by the flesh. Here, put off in the Greek could be translated "to put away from yourself." In other words, don't let these things be a part of your house. Tear out these rotten timbers and throw them away.

But merely tearing away the old is not enough; we must put something new in its place. God wants to do a work of transformation in your life. He is making you into a new man through the power of the Holy Spirit. The second half of verse 10 tells us how.

The key to the putting off and putting on process is the renewal of your mind. The process begins with a renewed focus on God. As we read the Word, we discover more and more about the God who saved us and who keeps us by His power. 2 Corinthians 3:18 tells us that as we look into the Bible we are exposed to God's glory, and it changes us internally. We are transformed to better see and to show His glory.

We can put some new man activities into our life, but if our mind isn't changed, we will eventually drift back to the fleshly acts of the old man. It would be like spraying air freshener over a can of rotten garbage. You might make the room smell better for a little while, but eventually the spray would dissipate, and the stink would come back. To fix the problem, the old bag of trash must be taken out, and a clean bag put in its place.

As God works through the Spirit to rid us of the works of the flesh, we must yield to the Spirit's working to bear fruit in our lives; otherwise, our final condition will be worse than where we started.

God's Glory—Our Treasure

(The Christian Adventure, Chapter 19)

Man's chief reason for existing is to glorify God. The only way in which God is glorified today is through individual believers' lives. If you do not glorify Him, He gets no glory. If you were the only Christian on earth, how much glory would God get?

God wants us to be happy! Christ never intended for the Christian life to be sad or boring. Yet, the real joy that exceeds all of the happiness that this world could ever offer comes only from a surprising source—a vibrant devotional life. Nothing is as exciting and energy producing as a dynamic and real prayer life. When one has a genuine prayer-and-Bible study-driven life, he feels better, is more active mentally, and experiences more joy and love than at any other time. Christ prays that all of us will know this joy, but God's glory, not our own happiness and joy, is to be our goal in life. This happiness and joy are byproducts of glorifying God.

God loves us with an everlasting love. In fact, He spends all of His time loving us and watching over us. A father has no greater joy than to watch his little child at play or to see his teenage son play ball or his daughter play the piano. His heart bursts with pride and love as he sits and watches his child succeed. Most fathers admit that they don't have enough time to enjoy this pleasure as much as they'd like. Yet, God—our heavenly Father—does nothing else but think of us, care for us, and watch over us. Do we break His heart by our actions? Or do we make His heart swell with joy and gladness as He sees us living lives of devotion to Him?

One day, we will share God's eternal glory in heaven. God, who created all things, thinks enough of His individual children that He plans for each of them to stay with Him forever. He longs for the day when we will be with Him.

We've seen that the Christian has no treasure on this earth. This world is not our home. Its enticements and allurements and promises of treasure are all empty and worthless. We're headed, instead, to heaven. Why should we try to enter its golden gates while wearing the clothes of this world, talking like its citizens, or thinking like they think?

May God help us to be faithful Christians, citizens of heaven who are longing to glorify our King and Father and to receive our everlasting inheritance in heaven.

The God of the Impossible

(The Inner Man, Chapter 4)

Certainly, God was the God of the great and faithful Abraham; of Moses, who talked with God and was great in Pharaoh's house; and of David, the young man who sought the Lord with all of his heart. But the God of Jacob?

Jacob could hardly be classified with these other spiritual giants. He was a scheming, deceitful, selfish, crooked, little worm. In fact, God Himself called him a worm (Isa. 41:14). This conniver caught his brother Esau in a weak moment and bargained him right out of his birthright. Not satisfied with that, he later conspired with his mother to trick his father into blessing him rather than Esau.

Incidentally, Jacob was not a youth when he deceived. Most Bible scholars think Jacob was a middle-aged man when he stole Esau's birthright, and he was perhaps over 80 when he cheated him out of his blessing.

Certainly, Jacob learned his wicked ways from a home that was far from ideal. His father Isaac wrapped his life and affections in his manly, masculine son Esau. A husky hunter, Esau would have been any father's delight. And Isaac was magnanimous, even willing to overlook Jacob's swindling ways and forgive him. Jacob's mother, Rebekah, on the other hand, focused her life on Jacob. She coddled and spoiled him. She taught him to scheme and helped him deceive his aging and nearly blind father.

Everything certainly seemed to be against Jacob's being God's choice to head a nation. But such is the way of God. He chose a worm that He might make him a prince! This fact demonstrates that no one is beyond being transformed and used by God. God is the God of the impossible.

The First Claim Principle

(*Behold Your God*, Chapter 35)

Jesus Christ has first claim on our lives because of who He is. That claim is intensified by what He has done for us. And finally, this claim is sealed by the fact that in salvation He purchased us. This CLAIM applies especially to five areas of our lives.

Calendar (Ps. 31:15; Luke 9:57–62)
Life (Matt. 6:33)
Affections (Col. 3:2; 2 Cor. 8:5)
Income (Prov. 3:9)
Minds (2 Cor. 10:5; Rom. 12:1)

Jesus Christ has first claim on our calendar (i.e., our time). That means that the first part of our day must go to Him and that the priorities of our schedule should reflect His lordship. We reflect His lordship not only by making our devotions the first priority of each day but also by causing the scheduled events of each day to reflect His priority. Does anything in your schedule hinder your relationship with Him? Does anything in your schedule take precedence over serving Him?

Here is a key point in our consideration of this principle. Jesus Christ has first claim on what you are to do in life! Sad to say, most of us use the pitiful excuse that we are going to do such and such or go to such and such a place to do such and such a job, but then we add, "If Christ wants me, He can have me." In other words, we assume that God doesn't want us or have us; therefore, we tentatively plan our lives in a secular world while saying that we are "willing" if He wants to use us. This is but an attempt to escape the reality of our responsibility to God. Once we understand the First-Claim Principle, however, we understand that He already has us and already wants us for His service! God created us for Himself. He saved us for His glory. He purchased us to serve Him!

The problem with separation and service lies in the heart, that is, with our affections. When one loves the Lord with all of his heart, mind, and soul, he will have little problem with the world. Our hearts do not have enough room for both love for the world and love for Christ. To fill our hearts with love for Him is to drive out any love for the world. When one considers who our Lord is, there is no doubt but that He must have first claim on those things that we love most.

The first fruit of what we earn is His. We always see the same pattern, whether we are talking about time, energy, education, vocation, hobbies, leisure time, or money: He is to be first. Hence, we see the importance of paying our tithe first—before we pay other bills or financial obligations. This principle goes contrary to the traditional self-employed businessman's advice to "Pay yourself first," but it's valid nonetheless.

The final area of Christ's claim on you is your mind. The battlefield of the Christian life is the mind. If Satan can get hold of our minds, he has us. If God has control of our minds, however, He has control of us. Who, then, controls your mind?

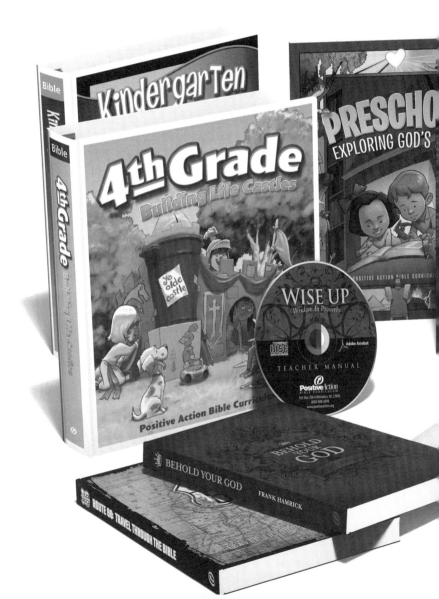

The passages in this book were taken from studies published by Positive Action Bible Curriculum (K4–12th grade). Our mission is to equip Bible teachers to magnify the majesty of God. For resources, curricula, and Bible studies visit us on the web at

www.positiveaction.org
or call us at (800) 688-3008.

Apples for Teachers
by Frank Hamrick

Apples are a traditional gift for schoolteachers, and it's our hope that this devotional will give you an "apple" a day of encouragement in your classroom ministry. Combining humor, love, and an insight gained from a life of teaching, Frank Hamrick challenges you to become a wise teacher.

Wisdom for Parents
by Frank Hamrick

Anyone who has been given the privilege of raising children knows that parenting requires great wisdom. Earthly wisdom is available everywhere you look, but in this devotional, Frank Hamrick challenges you to seek God's wisdom as you reflect His love to your children.

The Heart of the Matter: The God-Focused School
by Frank Hamrick

What do you really want for the young people in your school? Do you teach in hopes of modifying their behavior—or to transform their hearts?

The purpose of a Christian school is not to teach youth how to live, but to magnify the majesty of God. Christian school teachers are not behaviorists, but cardiologists. They teach, not only to encourage academic excellence, but also to challenge students to develop a heart for God and a zeal to exalt His name.

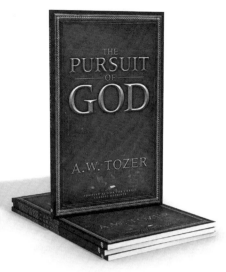

The Pursuit of God
by A. W. Tozer

In this book, A. W. Tozer declares that man can know, in a very personal way, our absolute, real, sovereign, eternal, majestic God. Like a child who takes her father's hand, we can fellowship with our God, learning from His power, grace, and love. This book urges the reader to look Godward and begin a lifelong pursuit of Him.

Christ Precious to Those That Believe
by John Fawcett

Reprinted by Positive Action, this classic work magnifies the beauty of Christ and His work. John Fawcett, an 18th century English pastor best known for his hymn "Blest Be the Tie that Binds," presents our Savior as an incomparable treasure. Without a desperate love for the Author of salvation, Fawcett argues, our obedience will remain defective. By God's grace, learn to magnify Christ in your life.

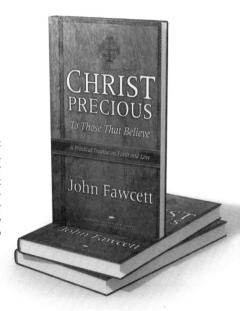

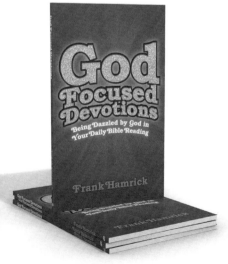

God Focused Devotions
by Frank Hamrick

When we go to the Word, we need to see more than just rules, stories, and precepts. We are supposed to see God in all His glory. In God Focused Devotions, you will learn the true goal of Bible reading—to focus your heart and mind on God. As you seek Him, He will transform you into Christ's image by the renewing of your mind. This devotional guide teaches the reader how to behold the majesty of God in His Word.